Third Eye Awakening

A Complete Guide to Awakening Your Third Eye and Developing Your Psychic Abilities

Jamie Parr

Table of Contents

Introduction 1

Chapter 1: What Is Your Third Eye? 3

Chapter 2: The Physical Third Eye 11

Chapter 3: The Different Psychic Abilities 14

Chapter 4: Methods for Awakening Your Third Eye 21

Chapter 5: Third Eye Awakening Meditation 31

Chapter 6: Developing Your Psychic Abilities 37

Chapter 7: Maintaining Your Third Eye Awakening 45

Chapter 8: When Your Third Eye Is Overactive 50

Chapter 9: When Your Third Eye Is Blocked 54

Chapter 10: Protecting Your Third Eye 58

Conclusion 68

Introduction

A third eye awakening was once an experience reserved only for those who had been initiated into it, or for those who were considered "chosen ones" as they had seemingly spontaneous awakenings. While it was commonly believed that anyone could awaken their third eye, most agreed that the only way to do so was to follow a highly specific path that would facilitate the awakening. Unless you were on that path, your third eye would remain closed and unusable.

Nowadays, we know that everyone has a third eye, and everyone has the capacity to awaken their third eye. Your third eye can be awoken through a traditional initiation, or it can be woken using many different third eye awakening practices that you can do yourself. Many have come to believe that, at one time, our third eyes were awake from birth and that they were an important part of our survival and livelihood. As the generations have gone by, we have slowly closed them as a result of living in a more modern, technological age. Instead of using our intuition and spirituality, people have grown to rely on technology and modern media to guide their decisions, moods, and behaviors.

Awakening your third eye can allow you to access incredible levels of energy. This awakened energy can be used for everything from deepening your connections to the world around you, to creating a profound relationship between yourself and whatever universal energies you discover through your third eye.

After generations upon generations of third eye awakenings, one thing we know for sure is that each person has a relatively unique experience. While the energy itself features many similarities from person to person, it also resonates with each individual in different ways. Upon experiencing a third eye awakening, people typically have a wonderful revelation and begin to perceive life and the universe differently than before.

In the following chapters we will discuss how you can facilitate your own third eye awakening so you, too, can tap into these deeper levels of experience. We will also discuss how you can awaken your third eye safely to avoid experiencing the unnerving symptoms of an overactive third eye chakra. Also, we will explain what kinds of new abilities and experiences you'll be able to access upon awakening your third eye.

Thank you for choosing this book. I hope you thoroughly enjoy learning all about third eye awakening!

Chapter 1: What Is Your Third Eye?

Your third eye is an energy center that every human has the ability to experience, and that can unleash incredible energy into your life. When used correctly, it can enhance your spiritual connection, bring you a deeper understanding of the world around you, increase your connection with others, and help you to feel a greater sense of personal peace. The third eye unlocks elements of truth that every human is searching for, whether it be a clearer understanding of why we all exist, or what the universe itself really is.

What Exactly Is the Third Eye?

Your third eye is the sixth energy meridian on a pillar of seven energy meridians located along your physical body, typically following the length of your spine. These energy meridians are known as chakras, and each one has its own unique energy signature and purpose. The third eye chakra, in particular, is located on your forehead directly between and slightly above your eyebrows. It is represented by the color indigo and carries an energy code that enables you to experience the unseen energies in the world around you, such as the energy of life itself.

On a practical, physical level, the third eye chakra is often represented by the pineal gland. It is said to be the chakra where you absorb energetic information from the world around you. This energy powers your spiritual intuition, which is housed in your third chakra, also known as the solar plexus chakra. Physically, the third eye chakra is nurtured using meditation or by interacting with things that are indigo in color, such as by wearing indigo colors on your body or consuming foods that are a deep blue color, such as blueberries.

On an emotional level, your third eye chakra creates a sense of unity between yourself and the world around you. This often creates an incredible sense of peace within individuals who have awakened their third eye chakra. When you realize that you are not separate from the world around you and that you share a deep, intimate connection with every living thing on earth, it creates an incredible sense of calm.

On a mental level, your third eye chakra allows you to know and see things that you did not previously see. Those with an awakened third eye chakra often carry a higher sense of maturity. Not in a sense that they know more than anyone else, but in that they realize they do not know more than anyone else and that they are truly no different than anyone else. There is no ego involved in this process. While they may see things from a heightened perspective and through the "eyes of awakening," those who have genuinely awakened their third eye chakra tend to have a more compassionate view of the world around them. This comes from having a higher understanding of the energy around them and the way that energy interacts with everyone, and everything.

Visually, your third eye chakra looks like an indigo ball of light rotating clockwise over your third eye chakra. When it is awakened and well-charged, your third eye chakra will have a vibrant color and energy to it. It will also have an easy time receiving information from the world around you without being overwhelming. When your third eye chakra is imbalanced, it will appear different and have different energies associated with it. We will talk in more detail about imbalanced third eye chakras in Chapter 8.

History of the Third Eye Chakra

Discussions of the third eye chakra first originated from spiritual traditions in India. There, Hinduism and Buddhism teachings included information about the third eye, explaining that the third eye was a chakra that represents one's enlightenment. The third eye chakra was activated, and enlightenment was achieved through meditation, as well as through yoga, which was used to help balance the mind, body, and spirit in preparation for meditation. In both Hinduism and Buddhism, the third eye chakra is said to be the "eye of consciousness," and when it is awakened, it enables people to see the world from an enlightened perspective.

Students of Kundalini and Zen teachings would often engage in specific practices to awaken their third eye chakra and enlighten themselves. Enlightenment was said to be the way that they could relieve themselves from human suffering and achieve a more peaceful state. Yoga and meditation were just the tip of the iceberg when it came to creating balance in their third eye chakras. Beyond that, they would also follow specific rules and guidelines in their lives that were said to eliminate Dharma or Karma so they would not actively sabotage their journey to enlightenment in their daily lives.

Discussions of the third eye have also been discovered in Chinese religious practices, as well as in Christianity. Outside of religion, philosophers have long discussed the third eye chakra and how this particular energy center works and connects people with enlightenment and the wonders of the universe. Over the years, many people have created their own ideas of what the third eye is, how it works, and why people should (or should not) awaken it within themselves.

In the late 1900s, Hindu peoples brought kundalini yoga and meditation to the West, which is when the topic of the third eye really took off in North America. Around that time, many people had begun questioning the American way of life and wanted to know if there was something more peaceful, spiritual, and soulful. Kundalini, and the awakening of the third eye chakra, brought that promise. Before long, Westerners were practicing Kundalini yoga and meditation, cultivating their own beliefs around the third eye chakra. Nowadays, third eye awakening is a popular topic attracting people from all walks of life. It has earned itself a seemingly permanent position in the mainstream narrative regarding spirituality, and rightly so!

Why the Third Eye Is So Popular

The third eye chakra has exploded in popularity primarily based on the fact that it activates a life experience that many are craving, but few know how to tap into. For generations, humans have been living primarily in the lower three chakras: the root chakra, the sacral chakra, and the solar plexus chakra. These three chakras, loosely summarized, govern survival, sexual reproduction, and instinct and intuition.

Now that we have reached a more advanced point in our evolution, we are ready to work with our higher chakras, including our heart chakras, throat chakras, third eye chakras, and crown chakra. The third eye chakra itself has become so popular because it provides seekers with access to specific information, answers, and energy that they seek and crave. Many claim that they have felt a deep need to tap into such energies from a young age. Experiencing an awakening enables these people to find the missing answers they seek, gain clarity, and feel a deeper sense of fulfillment and connection in their lives.

Another reason why the third eye has likely become so popular is that it sounds highly mystical and unusual to most. The idea of being able to tap into the unknown and "see" the unseen carries with it a sort of mystery that piques curiosity and leaves people wondering how they can access these energies themselves. This curiosity often leads to a lifelong journey of discovery, as the unintentional seeker finds more than they bargained for. At times, it can be overwhelming, so learning how to take this energy seriously and respect it for the powerful energy it is, is a necessary task.

The final reason why people have become fascinated with the third eye chakra is that, with proper practice, you can actually produce and release DMT naturally. DMT, or dimethyltryptamine, is a natural hormone within your body that is responsible for the creation of your dreams. Through intentional meditation exercises, one can train their brain to intentionally release DMT, which enables them to experience epic visions that many believe are filled with prophecy, truth, and codes for enlightenment. It should be forewarned that creating this experience takes time and is an experience that should be taken seriously, as it can be overwhelming and rather extreme for anyone who is not used to working with their third eye chakra.

The Biggest Mistake of Third Eye Awakenings

Before we dig deeper, I must warn you about the number one biggest mistake people routinely make when they are approaching their third eye awakening. This mistake has led to many people having negative and even traumatic experiences with their third eye, which has, at times, caused issues with mental health, anxiety, and even psychosis. While psychosis is an unlikely side effect of the third eye awakening, acute symptoms can and do occur around unexpected, unintentional, or uneducated awakenings.

The biggest mistake people tend to make when awakening their third eye chakra is that they do not take the awakening process seriously. Awakening your third eye chakra is powerful; you need to be extremely careful as it can take a person a lot of time to recover from their awakening.

The third eye chakra is full of powerful energy, and once it is awakened, you can never "un-see" what you saw and experienced. For the rest of your life, you will carry with you the visions and experiences you had upon awakening your third eye chakra, and that can have a serious impact on the quality of your life. If you want to have a positive experience and to be able to use your third eye for your benefit, you need to discover how you can positively use your third eye by first respecting it. You must acknowledge that, if you are not careful, your visions can be overwhelming and even seemingly dark or terrifying. These visions may interrupt your days with unexpected daydreaming, and your nights with nightmares. Even if they are not necessarily negative, they can become overwhelming and lead to you experiencing delusions that make it challenging to partake in standard, everyday life.

Going into your third eye awakening with the utmost respect for the energy that you will be tapping into is imperative to helping you have a positive experience. You can respect the energy by anticipating that it will be large and impactful, and by discovering how to safely balance and awaken your chakras. If you do that, awakening your third eye can be one of the most rewarding, positive, and life-changing things you can ever set out to do!

Chapter 2: The Physical Third Eye

Despite the third eye being a spiritual energy center, it has a physical location rooted within your very body. The pineal gland, located toward the center of your brain, is shaped like a small pinecone and is said to be responsible for the energy governed by the third eye. The pineal gland has been known to have a similar function as the third eye claims to have, though it is said that many are now living with a calcified or semi-calcified pineal gland, meaning it is not operating the way it was intended to. Some fear that if we are not careful, we may evolve away from having a pineal gland altogether.

Your pineal gland is responsible for secreting hormones that help your body govern its circadian rhythm, or sleep-wake cycles, and your reproductive hormones. This small gland helps you keep track of time, while also contributing to the timing of your sexual maturation. Melatonin, the primary hormone that is secreted by the pineal gland, also contributes to your ability to regulate stress and adapt to the changing world around you. Essentially, it plays a large role in your happiness and harmony.

Another hormone your pineal gland creates is DMT, or the hormone that is responsible for dreaming, as you have already learned. This naturally occurring substance allows for vivid visuals and psychic encounters, which directly correlate to the very purpose of the pineal gland itself. Many call this gland the doorway to God from within, declaring that through the secretion of DMT, you can visualize God and experience divine encounters. Others call the pineal gland the seat of the soul, claiming that this is the physical anchor point that keeps the soul rooted in the body.

You might be surprised to learn that humans are not the only ones with a pineal gland. The majority of animals also have pineal glands, and their glands work similarly to how a human's pineal gland works. In the past, philosophers and religious teachers falsely declared that humans were the only ones with the pineal gland, so it was surprising when scientists discovered that this is entirely untrue. It was discovered that animals typically have an even larger pineal gland than humans, which is attributed to them using theirs more frequently and not consuming things that contain chemicals that are known to repress the pineal gland. In humans, frequent consumption or use of food, water, and hygiene products like toothpaste that are rich with fluoride are said to calcify the pineal gland, which causes the gland to lie dormant, or partially dormant.

As the pineal gland remains unused, it becomes atrophied, and begins to waste away. This can be reversed by intentionally avoiding things that can calcify your pineal gland and by working with your third eye in meditation to intentionally draw energy to this gland and encourage the production of melatonin and DMT.

As you do this, you will naturally awaken the power of the pineal gland and access the psychic powers associated with your third eye.

Chapter 3: The Different Psychic Abilities

While people commonly talk about the five clairsenses, there are actually eight. The clairsenses refer to your senses beyond your physical senses and are directly responsible for your psychic abilities. "Clair" translates to "clear," meaning that these are your "clear" senses or your senses that can clearly pick up on sensory information from beyond the obvious tangible world around you. The information collected by your clairsenses is also picked up from the supernatural energy in your environment. Your ability to experience and decipher this information is directly related to your third eye and activity going on within this center of your body.

The eight clairsenses include clairvoyance, claircognizance, clairaudience, clairempathy, clairsentience, clairtangency, clairsalience, and clairgustance. Once your third eye is activated, it is said that you can experience any of these eight clairsenses, though it is most likely that you will only experience a couple that are particularly strong. If you prefer, though, you can work on strengthening each individual sense so you can use it as an additional way to experience spiritual energy and the world around you.

Clairvoyance

Clairvoyance is possibly the most well-known of the clairsenses, and it accounts for your ability to "clearly see" the world around you through your third eye. When you experience clairvoyance, you experience energy in the form of visions, dreams, mental images, or even mini movies that flash through your mind. Clairvoyants can often see the auras of plants, people, and animals, and they may also be able to see supernatural beings such as angels, ghosts, or other astral dimensional beings. Beyond their ability to see and visually interact with spirits, clairvoyants can often easily visualize anything they desire. This could be to manifest or visualize the solution to a problem they are facing. Often, clairvoyants are excellent with their sense of direction and their ability to solve visual problems. There are three types of skills a clairvoyant may have or use: precognition (the ability to see the future), cognition (the ability to illuminate the present), and post cognition (the ability to see the past.)

Claircognizance

Claircognizance refers to one's ability to clearly know something, often without a clear understanding of how they know it or where the information came from. Individuals who experience claircognizance often claim they "just know" and cannot pinpoint when that information came to them, or how. Claircognizant information is often called a "download" because those who have this particular skill believe the information has "downloaded" into their mind from source energy. Those who have claircognizance often feel as though information seems to nag at them or linger with them, illuminating something important such as a piece of information someone needs to know, or the reality that someone is lying when they claim to be telling the truth. Often, claircognizant people experience emotional or physical reactions to this information, which helps them understand the difference between a download and a personally developed idea or worry.

Clairaudience

Individuals who experience clairaudience, or clear hearing, are able to perceive sounds, noise, or even clear words from beyond the present realm. Those who primarily experience clairaudience claim that their number one interaction with the spiritual realm is through hearing, as they hear things using their inner voice. Some even claim that their inner voice sounds far different from their own voice, to the point where they can hear different distinctive voices related to the spirits they are picking up on. Clairaudient individuals may pick up on specific messages or information from the universe as a whole, or they may experience the reception of messages directly from supernatural beings. Common traits that clairaudient individuals share is that they experience an inner voice that tells them when to do something, or not do it, and they have an affinity with music or different sounds. Some can even hear the minute voice changes of an individual who is lying or trying to conceal something, even though almost no one else can hear it.

Clairempathy

With clairempathy or clear emotion, individuals are able to sense other's emotions, thoughts, and symptoms and may even feel them within their own physical body at times. However, not every individual will feel the emotions, thoughts, or feelings within their body; others may simply be aware of them without personally feeling them. This is the ideal situation, and with consistent effort, an individual who does personally take on other's symptoms can refrain from doing so through specific protective measures. Individuals will clairempathy often call themselves empaths, and they require self-care and psychic protection to shield themselves from the energetic overload they are prone to. The difference between clairempathy and clairsentience, which we are about to explore, is that empaths sense emotion while sentients experience the emotion for themselves.

Clairsentience

Clairsentient individuals, or those with clear physical feelings, can physically feel things within their bodies. Clairsentience is often described as a gut feeling, or an inner feeling that "something isn't right." Unlike clairempathy, where the feeler often has insight into what is going on, an individual with clairsentience often lacks this knowledge and simply feels that things are off within their body. You might feel that an environment is "off" or unsafe, feel the symptoms of another's pain or suffering, or even feel the hatred and pain of a traumatic or tragic event that took place in a specific area. A great example of a clairsentient experience would be if you were in a doctor's office and suddenly started feeling many different physical symptoms that were irrelevant to what you had booked your appointment for in the first place. In this case, you are likely taking on the physical symptoms of others in the office, sensing what the people around you are feeling.

Clairtangency

Clairtangency, or clear touching, is a unique experience whereby the feeler can sense information about something's past through touching it. For example, if you were to touch an old locket, you might start to have memories flood your mind from that locket's past, or the people who had owned the locket beforehand. People who experience clairtangency can often pick up the entire history of a person, place, or thing simply by touching it with their hands, which enables them to read the energy of said thing. Some people experience something similar to clairtangency, except they call it psychometry, which means to touch something and experience visions, emotions, or other sensations through the experience. Sometimes, they can pick up on this by being in the vicinity of an object without physically touching it. Because of how these experiences are perceived, some people are not convinced that clairtangency is a unique clairsense but is instead an experience of psychometry readings.

Clairsalience

Clairsalience, or clear smelling, is an experience where you can clearly smell things that are not in your immediate surrounding. For example, if you were driving down the road in your car and suddenly started smelling the ocean, even though you were extremely far away from the ocean, this would be clairsalience. Clairsalient individuals can often smell a variety of odors, from odors relating to memories or the memories of other people, to odors relating to the spirit or supernatural being that they are picking up on. Those who have a well-developed sense of clairsalience can often smell the energy around them, experiencing sweet-smelling or positive experiences when a situation is good, or experiencing negative smells or even sinus headaches when a situation is bad. Their ability to "smell energy" creates a powerful opportunity to pick up information about the world around them through their nose.

Clairgustance

Clairgustance, or clear tasting, is experienced by an individual who receives their psychic information through their sense of taste. When you can taste something despite not having recently consumed it, you are experiencing an episode of clairgustance. Some people will experience the taste of a favorite food of a deceased loved one, flavors related to certain crimes or information, or even the ability to "taste" the energy around them. To others, this may seem impossible. To those who experience it, it is challenging to describe; however, it does occur. Individuals who experience clairgustance often report experiencing flavors related to specific events or words, which give them unique energetic experiences as a result. Some may even enjoy specific energetic situations, words, or experiences because of the unique flavors they taste as a result.

Chapter 4: Methods for Awakening Your Third Eye

Awakening of the third eye can be achieved in many ways. Certain methods of awakening will directly awaken the third eye, while other methods of awakening will support more gradual awakening experiences. Some people experience gradual, gentle awakenings through healthy and regular behaviors performed with intention. For those who may be worried about being overwhelmed, this can be a great way to dip your toes in the water. However, if you want to experience a full awakening and the ability to work with and manage your third eye energy, you will need to undertake larger awakening practices such as meditation, yoga, reiki, and other forms of energy work.

Meditative Awakenings

Meditation is one of the most traditional ways to awaken the third eye. It directly works with clairvoyance, the most popular of the clairsenses, and provides you with the ability to visually become aware of, and work with, the energy associated with your third eye. Meditative awakenings are often achieved in three stages: the observation, the awakening, and the experience.

The observational stage of a third eye awakening is experienced during a meditative session where you simply observe the energy of your third eye chakra. This occurs whether you have awakened and worked with your third eye chakra in the past or not. The energy exists there and has been influencing your physical experience in one way or another. Becoming aware of your third eye chakra and the way it feels following all of your life experiences is a great opportunity to develop a "relationship" with the energy of your third eye. It also helps you become familiar with the energy so that when it comes to awakening and working with it intentionally, you feel confident in the energy you are working with. At this stage, you should not be trying to manipulate or work with your third eye at all; instead, you should merely observe the energy that exists there.

The awakening part of your meditative experience stands for the actual awakening itself. At this point, you set the intention of awakening your third eye chakra, and you activate the energy in a way that allows you to interact with and use it on purpose. Right now, you are not actually manipulating the energy or doing anything with it; you are simply asking it to become activated and setting the intention of being able to work with it in the future. As a result, the energy will begin to increase and become more prominent, and you will find yourself having more third eye experiences, and possibly some experiences associated with your clairsenses. You should be patient with this stage and let your third eye balance itself before you start working with the energy on purpose.

When you reach the part of your meditative awakening where you are ready to experience the third eye chakra in all its glory, you have arrived at the point where you can begin to work with your third eye energy intentionally. To reach this stage, your third eye chakra does not necessarily have to be balanced. Still, before intentionally working with your third eye you should feel comfortable and familiar with the energy that it contains. This way, you won't be overwhelmed with or confused by the energy that you are experiencing.

Awakening your third eye chakra through meditation will likely happen in many phases, as you awaken some energy, balance it, and awaken some more. Every person who uses this method will move back and forth between the observation, awaken, and experience stages several times over as they work toward deepening their awakening and magnifying their third eye experiences.

Yoga and the Third Eye

Yoga was originally developed as a way to harmonize the mind, body, emotion, and spirit so that a yogi could be fully prepared for meditation. A true yoga experience should include yoga that combines the physical movements of the body with the breath to create a balanced energy within the body. Following your yoga practice, you should sit in meditation for several minutes, or even hours if you wish to experience the third eye awakening.

These days, many varieties of yoga exist. Kundalini yoga is the best yoga to use when awakening the third eye chakra, though it is advised that you do kundalini yoga with an experienced practitioner who can aid you in the energetic experiences you have. Kundalini yoga will awaken massive energy within you. Not just within your third eye but within all of your chakras. This release of energy facilitates what is known as a kundalini awakening. Having an experienced guide to teach you about the different phases of the awakening and to help you navigate your experiences ensures that you will be able to do so safely, and without being overwhelmed.

Once you have activated your third eye, yoga is an excellent way to keep it balanced as it physically moves your energy around. This means that stagnant energy will be moved out, and excessive energy will be carefully balanced. The best way to view yoga as a part of the awakening experience is to see it as a form of physical enlightenment that creates the perfect foundation for an energetic and spiritual enlightenment to follow. This way, your enlightenment is balanced and grounded within the body. Any awakening that happens in an ungrounded body *will* cause energetic chaos and overwhelm for the individual experiencing the energy itself.

Reiki Charged Awakenings

Reiki is a popular form of energy work that was derived from a Japanese practitioner who believed in the chakras and their ability to have a magnificent impact on the body, mind, emotions, and soul. This energy work is typically done unto a person by an accredited practitioner who has been taught to do reiki on others. Some will also learn to do reiki themselves and will use their reiki skills to awaken and balance their own energy, too. If you plan on doing continuous work with your chakras, you might like to find a trained reiki practitioner, or become trained in this practice yourself. Reiki is the most gentle, subtle way to work within your energy field to create awakenings and balance, though it can have a rather intense impact on some people.

The best way to awaken your third eye through reiki is to have a professional practitioner do this with you. That way, you can focus entirely on your awakening and allow the practitioner to work within your energy field. Being able to fully surrender to the experience and release your need to control is an excellent way to allow yourself to fully observe, awaken, and experience your third eye chakra. Before you do this, however, ensure that you are working with a practitioner that you trust and who fully understands the gravity of awakening your third eye chakra.

Another way that you can infuse reiki into your awakening experience is to include it as a supportive measure. You can see a reiki practitioner on a regular basis, use crystals, essential oils, candles, or incorporate other tools into your meditation or yoga practices. These tools can be used to assist you in balancing and elevating your energy, further enhancing your awakening.

Intentional Energy Work

While reiki is considered the gentlest and most popular form of energy work, there are other forms of energy work that can be used on your chakras, too. Some forms of energy work, such as Qigong, therapeutic touch, healing touch, or Emotrance, are specifically constructed forms of energy work that are designed to create specific results in your energy centers.

Aside from specifically designed energy working modalities, there are also certain practitioners who "freestyle" their energy work. This means they have activated their own clairsenses and ability to work within the energy field, and they have created their own unique modality that uses their signature techniques to work on other's energy. These modalities can be wonderfully unique and personal, though you do have to be careful as you do not want to work with someone who may have poor intentions for you. Be sure you can completely trust the person who is doing your energy work before receiving a session from them.

If you choose to use one of the many other forms of energy work to awaken your third eye, you must research that modality and understand it first. Pick the modality that resonates most with you so you can receive an awakening that serves your best interest. If you are unsure of which resonates most, try meditating and asking yourself, first, to see what calls to you. This is an excellent way to get used to working with energy within yourself and trusting your own intuition when it comes to your energetic experiences. You can also use this method to help you identify which practitioner would be best for you to work with, so that you can choose one who meshes well with you and your needs.

Third Eye Food and Beverage

While food and beverage alone will not facilitate a third eye awakening, you can use food and beverage as a way to support your third eye awakening. When using food, beverages, and other edible products, you need to ensure you are using ones that are effective for the third eye chakra.

The best foods to eat for the third eye include blue, black, and purple foods such as blackberries, blueberries, purple cabbage, purple carrots, eggplants, grapes, purple kale, and purple sweet potatoes. If you come across any other foods that come in a nice purple color, you can eat those, too. Because the brain and the third eye chakra are so closely linked, salmon, walnuts, avocado, and other omega-3 rich foods that are good for brain function are also excellent for the third eye.

For beverages, you can consume purple drinks, such as blueberry or blackberry juice or tea. Making purple-based smoothies out of all of the foods mentioned above is also a great way to ensure that you positively nourish your third eye chakra.

Beyond foods and beverages, some spices and herbs can be used to help your third eye chakra as well. Teas made of blackberry, eyebright, bilberry, blueberry, chamomile, lavender, schisandra, ginkgo, or amaranth are excellent for your third eye chakra. Each of these either supports your third eye through their energy, or through the fact that they support brain health, which aids your third eye chakra. Cooking with spices such as rosemary, sage, thyme, and vanilla is excellent for your third eye, too.

Third Eye Tools

Third eye tools include anything you can use on a regular basis without having to physically eat or drink anything. Essential oils, bath products, and meditational tools are all great examples of third eye tools. Each tool has its own unique way of being used with the third eye chakra to facilitate your awakening.

For essential oils, you can use scents such as camphor, chamomile, cedarwood, eucalyptus, geranium, lavender, musk, myrrh, rosemary, rosewood, sage, tea tree, thyme, and vanilla. You can also blend any of these together to create an excellent scent for your diffuser to be used while you are meditating or practicing yoga. If you are on the go, try making a roller stick to help you awaken or balance your third eye chakra while you're out and about. A great third eye blend of cedarwood, rosewood, and vanilla smells delicious and works perfectly for your third eye chakra.

Bath products that are made of these scents, or that contain crystals, are excellent for your third eye, as well. You can also use color therapy by using bath products that are indigo in color, as these will greatly assist your third eye chakra in awakening. If you prefer to use color therapy to assist with awakening your third eye, you can try scarves, clothes, or even color therapy glasses, all of which are designed to help you infuse your life with more of the third eye energy. The third eye is linked with indigo, so make sure that you are incorporating this color into your life in as many ways as possible.

Crystals that are associated with the third eye chakra include ammonite, amethyst, angelite, apophyllite, azurite, blue calcite, blue tigers, celestite, coquina jasper, crazy lace agate, dumortierite, fluorite, hypersthene, iolite, labradorite, lapis lazuli, moonstone, sodalite, tanzanite, and tournalinated quartz. You can meditate with these crystals, wear them as jewelry, or infuse your essential oils or room sprays with them as a way to increase the energy of these crystals in your space. Keeping these crystals in your space by laying them around your room or keeping one near your pillow can be useful.

Chapter 5: Third Eye Awakening Meditation

A third eye awakening meditation, as you might have guessed, happens in three stages: the observation, the awakening, and the experience. I encourage you to wait to practice the awakening and experience meditations until you feel completely comfortable with the observational stage. Before you do the awakening and experience meditations, ensure you are fully aware of how to work with an overactive and blocked chakra so you can adjust your chakra energy as needed. It may also be helpful to have an experienced reiki practitioner or yogi who can help you navigate the awakening in a more peaceful, balanced manner. Remember, the biggest mistake you can make is not respecting the awakening enough, so be patient and be aware of how intense this energy can be.

The Observational Meditation

Begin your observational meditation by either sitting with your legs crossed and your hands palm-up on your knees, or by lying down with your arms and legs completely relaxed. Choose whichever position you find to be the most comfortable. Keep a long, straight spine and square shoulders. Allow your eyes to grow heavier as you start to breathe deeply into your diaphragm, encouraging your breath to relax without trying to control it in any way. Simply observe your breath.

As you start to feel relaxed, allow your eyes to completely close, and draw your awareness to your personal energy. Feel your energy circulating through your body, creating a sense of calm and peace within yourself. Notice if your energy seems overactive or underactive anywhere. Focus on those areas where energy seems either overactive or underactive, and simply acknowledge those sensations without trying to manipulate or change them.

Now, move your focus up to your third eye. You may wish to turn your eyes inward and slightly up to look toward the energy in your third eye, as you turn your awareness here. As you do, observe the energy that lingers in this space. You may see, feel, sense, or simply become aware of the existence of energy. Whatever you do, do not try to manipulate the energy, as your only goal right now is to observe it and experience it for what it is.

When you are done, draw your awareness back into your body, then into the room around you, and awaken yourself to the present moment. Give yourself a few minutes to come back from your observational experience before going back to your daily activities fully. You may wish to journal about your experience at this point so you can keep track of your evolution and experience as time goes on.

Repeat this meditation exercise regularly and observe the energy of your third eye chakra for several days or weeks and how it feels and changes. When you start to feel deeply comfortable with your third eye chakra, both within meditation and afterwards, you are ready to move on to the awakening meditation.

The Awakening Meditation

The awakening meditation is once again best performed while sitting with your legs crossed and your hands facing palm-up on your lap, or while laying down with your legs and arms completely relaxed and your palms up. Keep your spine straight, your shoulders square, and look straight ahead.

When you are ready, draw your awareness to your breath and use your breath to begin calming yourself down. Feel yourself sinking into a state of relaxation as your breath naturally slows and deepens, drawing into your diaphragm and releasing completely. As you start to relax even more deeply, close your eyes and draw your awareness into your body, scanning for how you feel in this present moment.

When you start to feel at one with yourself, you can begin to draw your awareness up to the familiar energy of your third eye. Spend several moments observing it and experiencing that day's energy, allowing yourself to feel restful and comfortable in this space. Then, invite your third eye chakra to awaken. Set the intention for a gentle, compassionate, loving awakening experience to occur, and feel your energy gradually begin to shift and awaken. You may feel a rush of energy unfold within your third eye, or you may feel nothing at all. Either one is perfectly okay. So long as you continue to hold the intention for a loving, gentle awakening, your third eye will begin to awaken more with each meditation session you have.

Once your third eye has spent time awakening, resume your observation by simply becoming aware of what is happening and what it feels like. Allow yourself to enjoy this intimate space with yourself and your personal energy for as long as you would like, before bringing your awareness back into your body, then into the room around you. Gently awaken yourself from your meditation and give yourself plenty of time to relax and journal before resuming your day to day activities.

Do as many awakening meditations as you feel inclined to in order to reach your desired level of awakening, but do not exceed what feels comfortable for you as you do not want to create a traumatic and overwhelming experience. You can always awaken your third eye further in the future, as there is no rush to awaken all of your energies at once.

The Experience Meditation

The experience phase comes in when you are ready to start using your third eye intentionally. It is easiest to do the experience meditation by either holding an object that you will work with, or by closing your eyes and working with your visualizations. If you wish to close your eyes and work through visualization, simply repeat the awakening meditation, but invite your energy to show you a unique vision through your third eye. If you wish to experience the third eye in practice, the following meditation will help you work with a specific object, such as a crystal, a vintage piece of jewelry, or an image.

Start your meditation by sitting cross-legged with your spine straight and your shoulders square. Either hold the object in front of you or place it on a surface that is close to eye-level. Then, begin meditating on it by relaxing your gaze on the object and drawing your breath deeper with each cycle, allowing you to deepen your state of awareness. Begin by checking in with your personal energy and connecting deeply to it, becoming aware of how you are feeling and how your energy is moving within your body.

When you are ready, draw your awareness up into your third eye, and then out into the object you are holding, as if you are making an energetic link between your third eye and the object. Invite information to be perceived by your third eye, allowing it to come in whatever way feels natural for you. You may see, feel, hear, taste, smell, sense, or experience something that provides you with increased information about the object you are holding.

After you have received information, allow yourself to draw your awareness back into your third eye. Focus on the energy you feel in your third eye and release any energy that does not belong to you. When you are ready, you can release yourself from this experience and awaken back into the room around you. Give yourself several moments to come back, and journal about your experience if you desire.

You may repeat this practice anytime you like, but be sure to give yourself time in between sessions to balance your energies and come back to a state of grounded existence before trying again. Rushing this process can lead to an overwhelming experience.

Chapter 6: Developing Your Psychic Abilities

As you continue to awaken your third eye, you will find that your psychic abilities naturally improve with each meditation session. Each individual has their own set of abilities that are naturally stronger than the others, and these will be the abilities you experience more intensely during these meditations. However, you can awaken your other abilities if you desire to deepen these psychic senses even further.

Before you begin awakening your other psychic senses, it helps to deepen the senses you are already experiencing and to draw them into a state of natural balance. In doing so, you ensure that you can safely rely on these senses to guide you in the process of awakening and developing your other psychic senses. Further, your natural psychic senses can be further developed over time, making them even stronger and more attuned to your energy and the world around you. When it comes to psychic development, there is never an end to the learning and growing process.

Identifying and Deepening Your Natural Psychic Senses

Your natural psychic senses should be easy to identify once you have begun the awakening process, as they will be the ones that naturally start to activate during your psychic experiences. You might experience these senses exclusively during meditation, or you might start experiencing them out in the world in your day to day experiences. For example, if you are naturally inclined to experience clairempathy, you may start intuitively picking up on the energy and feelings of everyone around you, even when you are not trying to do so. As you learn to develop your psychic senses, you will discover how to either pay closer attention to this or stop it from happening if you feel it becomes overwhelming.

The natural psychic senses that develop during your awakening and experiencing process will deepen on their own as you continue to observe, awaken, and experience your third eye. You may even realize that you had already been experiencing those senses before your intentional awakening, but that they become sharper and more prominent following your awakening. It is important that you continue to work on these specific senses as you go. These senses will assist you in developing your secondary senses by helping you more accurately perceive different pieces of energetic information. Essentially, they begin to work as your "guide" in the development of your other psychic senses and abilities.

Developing Your Secondary Psychic Senses

Some people are perfectly happy having only their primary senses activated, or the ones that come naturally to them. For some who awaken their third eye, they experience one or two primary senses, and that is it. They have no desire to awaken any further senses because they are satisfied with the information they are receiving from these primary senses and trust that they are receiving plenty of information as it is. For others, they may want to awaken their secondary senses, or any additional senses, as a way to deepen their readings and increase their accuracy. You may wish to awaken one or all of your secondary senses. There is no right approach for this, though it is advised that you take it just one ability at a time to avoid overwhelming yourself and creating an overactive chakra. Keeping your chakras balanced ensures that you have a positive, productive experience with your third eye at all times.

Clairvoyance

Clairvoyance is easily developed by increasing your imaginative abilities, as this is where your clairvoyance abilities exist, also. Spending time daydreaming, visualizing objects you have recently looked at, or visualizing your desires with as many details as possible improves your clairvoyant abilities. The more you develop your imagination, the easier it is to draw on your clairvoyance and use it.

To practice developing your clairvoyance for readings, you can start by holding an object in your hand and observing it carefully. Then, close your eyes and try to picture that object within your mind's eye. Once you have, set the intention to "see" the energy of that object using your mind's eye. You may see an aura, symbols, or other symptoms of energy appearing in your mind surrounding the object, or replacing the object, as you begin to experience clairvoyance. Practice this regularly if you want to strengthen your clairvoyant abilities.

Claircognizance

Developing your clear knowing ability comes from giving yourself permission to let your inner walls down and receive knowledge from the objects around you. A great way to practice developing claircognizance is to hold an object in your hand and, without encouraging any of your other senses, practice receiving information from it. Ideas will begin to pop in your mind about where it came from, who touched it previously, or what energy is associated with it, and you will be able to receive information through these ideas. You must practice trusting these ideas as they pop into your mind, as the automatic thoughts are typically claircognizance, but they can be overridden by overthinking forced thoughts, or thoughts of doubt. A relaxed, trusting mind is the best way to develop your claircognizance.

Clairaudience

Clairaudience is one of the few psychic abilities that can be quite challenging to develop, and many never successfully do. With clairaudience, the experience is different from hearing your own inner voice; instead, you hear the voices of others', or sounds that are completely unrelated to your own inner voice but provide insight into a certain energetic event. For example, some individuals with clairaudience experience the sound of angel bells or can hear high pitched hums coming off of certain crystals when they hold them. You can encourage clairaudient experiences by meditating and inviting a clairaudient experience to occur. Those who experience clairaudience claim that the more you let go of your control over the experience, the more likely you are to hear messages or sounds through clairaudience.

Clairempathy

Clairempathy can be developed by spending time around others, and intentionally tuning in to their feelings and experiences, ideally without first asking what they are feeling and experiencing. A great way to practice is to scan someone else's body and sense any energy you can pick up on, which may indicate something they are feeling or experiencing within themselves. Once you have picked up on something, place that within your awareness and see if you can identify if this feeling is true or not, either by directly asking if it is appropriate, or by observing through conversation and experience.

Clairsentience

Clairsentience is something not many wish to experience, as the awakening of clairsentience can lead to the development of unwanted physical symptoms as you literally begin to feel how other people are feeling. If you do wish to do this, however, you can do so by observing the energy of others and setting the intention for a mirrored experience to occur within yourself. Then, allow for your own energy to mirror the energy of someone else, as you pick up on their symptoms. Often, medical mediums or the medically intuitive will do this as a way to identify where an individual may be suffering within their body and what might actually be going on with them, particularly when conventional doctors have failed to discover the problem. It is extremely important that you release the mirrored effect and build an energetic shield following these experiences to ensure that others' energy is promptly removed from your body and not lingering there, wreaking havoc on your own wellbeing.

Clairtangency

To increase your clairtangency, you want to practice holding objects in your hand and intuitively receiving information about those objects. The easiest way to do this is to start by actually purchasing an oracle deck or a tarot deck and doing your intuitive readings with these. You could also use crystals or other tools that already have designated meanings. The idea is to use spiritually charged devices that already have assigned meanings so that you can check in with the meanings after your intuitive channeling and identify if you were accurate or not. To do this, hold one of the devices in your hand and begin channeling information about what it means, and what its energy archetype is. Once you have absorbed your information, you can look for the actual meaning of that tool to identify what it means and compare your understanding to the original one. As you continue practicing with different tools, you will find yourself better interpreting the energy you are picking up on from each tool.

Clairsalience

Clairsalience, or clear smelling, can be cultivated best by closing your eyes and recalling specific scents from your past. For example, let's say you smell a beautiful flower, and it triggers a happy, peaceful memory for you. Later, you can meditate and focus on recalling that scent to see if you can bring it back into your awareness and experience it once more. Continue doing this over and over until you can smell the memory, or the flower itself, simply by thinking about it. Over time, you will find yourself smelling a variety of things, from memories to different energies, and picking up on information through your olfactory system.

Clairgustance

Clairgustance, or clear taste, is quite different from any other clairsense. Like with clairaudience, it is a more challenging one to develop because it is usually either something you naturally experience or something you do not. If you do want to try to develop this clairsense, you can do so by attempting to recall the flavor of something you ate recently. Continue practicing until you can taste it, at which point you have activated clairgustance. You can also work on "tasting" energy by keeping yourself open to the experience of recognizing the various tastes in your mouth and scanning to understand what the energetic associations of these tastes are. Over time, you may find that certain tastes indicate certain energetic experiences for you.

Chapter 7: Maintaining Your Third Eye Awakening

As you begin to awaken your third eye, there are many different practices you will need to take on to maintain your awakening and maintain your health through your awakening. Like the experience of having a body requires physical self-care, or the experience of having a mind and emotions requires mental and emotional self-care, the experience of awakening your third eye requires spiritual self-care. Adequate self-care measures will help ensure that you have a positive experience with your third eye awakening, without becoming overwhelmed or burnt out.

Physical Self-Care for the Third Eye

Physical self-care for your third eye is largely done through diet, exercise, and massage. Consuming foods that are known for purifying and balancing your third eye, such as the purple foods we discussed previously, is an excellent way to balance your third eye through diet.

Exercise enables you to effectively release any energy that has built-up in your body as a result of your third eye, which is common when you are absorbing information and energy from the external world. Yoga is one of the most powerful forms of physical exercise when it comes to releasing energy from your body and balancing yourself and your third eye. Specific yoga poses such as child's pose, alternate nostril breathing, and candle gazing are excellent for your third eye chakra.

Massage can be used to help balance your third eye chakra, especially when using heavily diluted essential oils such as chamomile and lavender on your third eye chakra. Take a single small drop of your massage oil and massage your forehead, all the way to your temples, to help balance the energy in your third eye. This is an extremely relaxing experience that can help release any energy that may be built up in your third eye while gently encouraging it to expand.

Mental Self-Care for the Third Eye

The third eye can trigger powerful mental experiences, especially visions. Upon initially awakening your third eye, you may find that you experience prominent visions during the day and intense dreams at night. You might even wake up feeling exhausted because you did not sleep well due to the fact that your dreams were so active. Taking proper care of your mind ensures that you are balancing your third eye in a healthy, effective manner.

The best form of mental self-care is achieved through mindset, which enables you to relieve your fear and maintain a sense of confidence, curiosity, and certainty around your third eye. Your goal is to ensure that you do not allow fear or doubt to infiltrate your mind, as in doing so, you allow these feelings to grow, and that can increase your likelihood of experiencing negative energies in your third eye chakra. If you notice fear or doubt developing, do not grow fearful of these emotions; instead, become confident that you will be safe and encourage yourself to focus more on enjoying a positive experience. This way, you are more likely to experience peace and comfort with your third eye, rather than increased anxiety and overwhelm.

To develop confidence in your third eye, become aware of the power in your third eye, and have a healthy respect for that energy and power. Develop your confidence in your ability to enjoy positive experiences with your third eye, your ability to protect yourself, and the peace you have access to on a continuous basis. By simply choosing peace, you increase your likelihood of experiencing peace and enjoying comfort in your third eye and related energies. Two simple practices that can help with mindset are: saying daily affirmations, and having a gratitude practice where you acknowledge all of the positive things in life that you are grateful for. Doing these two simple things daily can greatly influence your mood, mindset, and energy.

Emotional Self-Care for the Third Eye

Because of how much energy you will be perceiving and experiencing through your third eye, you may experience an overwhelming amount of emotions associated with your awakening, too. These emotions can come from others' energy, the increased energy itself, or even as a reaction to the symptoms of your awakening, such as visions or other clairsensory experiences.

The best way to engage in emotional self-care is to spend time meditating *without* working with your third eye during those meditations. Instead, meditate while you create space for yourself to observe and work through your emotions, without trying to manipulate or control them. Often, becoming aware of and releasing your energy in this way enables you to let go of your emotions fully. You can also meditate while doing yoga if you want to physically move your emotions out of your body, as this may provide additional relief.

Spiritual Self-Care for the Third Eye

Since your third eye awakening is a largely spiritual experience, it is important that you take care of your spiritual energy during your awakening, and after, too. You can take care of your spiritual energy using methods such as reiki, crystal healing, meditation, or other forms of energy balancing.

Another great way to take care of yourself during the awakening experience is to wear crystal jewelry or carry crystals in your pocket as a way to help you stay safe from negative energy. Crystals like amethyst, smoky quartz, moldavite, and black obsidian are excellent for protecting your third eye. You can also wear a diffuser necklace or bracelet and dab it with an essential oil known for protecting the third eye, such as lavender or cedar, as a way to protect and balance your energy on the go.

Chapter 8: When Your Third Eye Is Overactive

Overactive chakras can cause traumatic experiences for people who have them, because they can bring with them an array of overwhelming symptoms. Whenever you hear of someone having a negative experience with their third eye chakra, it is often because they had an overactive third eye, which resulted in them having seemingly uncontrollable clairsensory experiences. Overactive third eye chakras are most common when you are first awakening your third eye because you are experiencing a sudden influx of energy into this part of your body for the first time. Knowing how to prevent and heal an overactive third eye ensures that you are ready to deal with this the moment it starts, meaning you will be far less likely to have a negative experience with your third eye.

Identifying an Overactive Third Eye

Your overactive third eye chakra can manifest through physical and non-physical symptoms. Physically, you might experience headaches, vision problems, seizures, insomnia, nausea, or sinus issues. These symptoms should never be taken lightly and should always be inspected by a doctor *before* you rule them as being the result of your third eye awakening. If, however, these symptoms are unusual and cannot be traced back to a medical root cause, they are likely the result of your overactive third eye chakra.

Aside from physical symptoms, you may also experience hallucinations, anxiety, mental fog, overwhelm, paranoia or delusions, or a tendency to be more judgmental than normal. These symptoms can be the result of you experiencing far too much feedback from your third eye chakra, which leads to you feeling uncomfortable and imbalanced. Healing your overactive third eye chakra will help you stop experiencing these unwanted symptoms.

A Meditation for Balancing Your Overactive Third Eye

The first and most productive route of action to take when your third eye is overactive is to engage in a balancing meditation. This type of meditation is intended to calm the energies of this chakra and create more harmony in your energy centers. To do a balancing meditation for an overactive third eye, start by engaging in a typical meditation. Either sit with your legs crossed and your hands palm-up on your thighs, or lay down with your legs and hands relaxed by your sides. Keep your spine straight and shoulders square, and focus on your breath.

As you advance through your meditation, use your breath to direct calm energy into your third eye by exhaling excess energy, and inhaling relaxing energy. Each time you breathe in, visualize calming energy moving through your third eye and regulating the chakra, and each time you exhale, visualize excess and unwanted energy being released. Do this over and over until you start to feel a deeper sense of peace in your energy field.

Tools to Balance Your Overactive Third Eye

Tools are an excellent way to balance your overactive third eye if you are looking for a long-term approach to balancing your energies. At this point, using energy healing modalities like reiki may be too overwhelming, possibly causing you to experience even more energy in your third eye before you experience relief. Instead of using tools like reiki, use tools that are designed to ground and release your energy as quickly as possible.

Black obsidian is a great tool you can utilize. It is possibly the best stone to use for your overactive third eye. It can absorb the overactive energy and release it from your energy field rapidly. Once you have released the energy, use something like amethyst or smoky quartz to prevent your third eye from becoming overactive once again.

Recovering from the Symptoms of an Overactive Third Eye

While the process of rebalancing an overactive third eye chakra is often discussed, recovering from an overactive third eye chakra is rarely talked about. The experiences you have as a result of an overactive third eye chakra can be overwhelming or even traumatic for some. Hallucinations, delusions, and paranoia, in particular, can be troubling to experience and can make the idea of working with your third eye in the future seem inconceivable. You might be afraid of having the same experiences again, which can actually aggravate your energy and leave you at risk of having another negative experience. The best way to proceed is to allow yourself to first heal from the overactivity and gain perspective from it so you can understand why it happened and release your fear and anxiety. Then, start the awakening process again from the very beginning and take care not to overwhelm your energy this time. If you need to, consider working with a mentor or guide who can help you ease back into the experience in a more positive way. The best course of action is a combination of modalities. Ideally, you would combine a meditation practice with a healthy diet, exercise such as yoga, the use of crystals, and possibly the assistance of an energy healer or mentor.

Chapter 9: When Your Third Eye Is Blocked

A blocked third eye is, as you'd likely expect, the exact opposite of an overactive third eye. Unlike an overactive third eye which creates feelings of overwhelm and hyperactivity, a blocked third eye can actually prevent you from using your third eye chakra properly. People who have yet to awaken their third eye are typically experiencing a blocked third eye and are unable to receive proper feedback from this energy center. Many people do not experience *any* feedback from this energy center at all, which can be just as negative as experiencing too much energy.

Often, especially after you have already intentionally awakened your third eye chakra, if you experience a blockage it will be related to an unwanted or overwhelming experience you had with your third eye. For example, if you experienced too much energy through your third eye, or had an unwanted vision, you might purposefully or subconsciously block your third eye as a way to protect yourself from having another unwanted experience. Once you have blocked your third eye, you must intentionally unblock it if you wish to experience free-flowing energy there again. If you are attempting to awaken your third eye in the first place and are having trouble fully awakening it, you may also be experiencing a blockage.

Identifying a Blocked Third Eye

A third eye chakra that has been blocked can cause both physical and non-physical symptoms, just like an overactive third eye can. The physical symptoms you might experience include difficulty sleeping, headaches, or pressure in the middle of your forehead. Your non-physical symptoms might include confusion or anxiety, especially around decision making, a lack of imagination, indecisiveness around your future, poor memory, or a deep inner urge to meditate and spend more time with yourself.

When your third eye has been blocked as a reaction to overactive energy, the way to awaken it is not to overactive your energy once more. Instead, it is to recognize the need for calm energy and to awaken the third eye through a calm, gradual approach. This way, you honor your chakra's need for a peaceful and gentle experience, while reawakening yourself to the abilities of your third eye.

A Meditation for Balancing Your Blocked Third Eye

Meditating to balance a blocked third eye is different from meditating to calm an overactive third eye, as there will be far less frantic energy involved in your blocked third eye. Further, you do not want to introduce frantic energy to it, as this is likely why it has become blocked in the first place.

An observational and awakening meditation is the best way to approach your blocked third eye, as this helps you gently draw more energy into your energy center. You can also meditate on a mantra such as "I invite my third eye to awaken gently," or "I awaken my third eye with gentleness and confidence," both of which can help you encourage your third eye to become unblocked. Breathe deeply throughout the experience and be patient with yourself as you find your way back to an unblocked state of being.

Tools to Balance Your Blocked Third Eye

If your third eye has become blocked, the best tools for awakening your third eye once more include frankincense, myrrh, or essential oils massaged into your forehead, as well as crystals that you can use to balance your energy. There are many different crystals you can use to unblock your third eye chakra. You can wear them, or better yet, you can lay down and place them over your third eye as you meditate.

The ten best crystals for awakening your third eye chakra are: amethyst, clear quartz, labradorite, lapis lazuli, moldavite, sodalite, moonstone, iolite, Herkimer diamond, and unakite jasper. All of these can be worn, meditated with, or kept in your general vicinity to encourage your energy to awaken and increase in your third eye once again.

Recovering from the Symptoms of a Blocked Third Eye

While recovering from an overactive chakra requires you to come to terms with the overwhelming experiences you had, recovering from a blocked third eye requires you to be extremely gentle with yourself. You might experience a range of emotions, from anxiety or fear around the experience, to grief around having lost your abilities in the first place. Accepting these feelings ensures that you are able to be at peace with yourself and your experiences, and this will create space for you to heal from them so you can feel more confident in awakening your third eye chakra.

Recovering from a blocked chakra is not all that different from recovering from an overactive chakra, since they often have a similar root cause. One simply means you have not balanced the overactive energy, while the other means you were likely traumatized or overwhelmed by the activity and shut it off instead of balancing it. Rebuilding your confidence in yourself and your third eye will help you experience peace from your blockage and develop the willingness to work with your third eye once again.

Chapter 10: Protecting Your Third Eye

The final element you need to learn about before you can safely activate your third eye chakra is how to protect your third eye. Protecting yourself from overactivity or blockages is important, as is knowing what to do if you do end up having either of these energetic experiences. However, there is far more that goes into your third eye that can affect your wellbeing than just overactivity and blockages.

When you start developing your psychic abilities, you are susceptible to having a wide range of energetic experiences through these senses. You may experience energy from everyone around you, from the space around you, the memories within that space, or even from entities that you may or may not be able to see. These different energy sources can be overwhelming, especially if you are not used to experiencing them. Further, you could end up receiving unwanted energy from those around you, which can be a very negative experience.

Knowing how to protect your third eye means you can create energetic boundaries that prevent you from absorbing unwanted energy through your third eye. This way, you are less susceptible to dangerous psychic attacks or energy, and you are more open to having positive, wanted experiences. It is important that you continue to protect yourself on a day to day basis, and that you protect yourself extra on days when you intend to work with your third eye. This way, you will only experience positive, protected, and intentional experiences with your third eye.

Protect Yourself through Your Dreams

While your dreams can become overactive and even overwhelming after awakening your third eye chakra, it is important that you do not allow these energies to get too out of control. Firstly, overactive dreams are an indication that your third eye energy is too high and that you need to balance it.

Second, you need to observe what is actually happening in your dreams, as this will help indicate what you are experiencing on an energetic level, which can shed light on how you can help balance yourself once more. Like with anything, it is always easier to facilitate a third eye healing when you know where the imbalance lies and what, specifically, needs to be healed.

A great way to keep track of your dreams and your third eye energy is to keep a dream journal. Write in your dream journal every morning, taking note of any dreams you had, the emotions they elicit, and what you think they mean. If you take measures to balance your energy or heal yourself from an imbalance following a dream, document it, and keep track of how well those methods did or did not work. This way, you can keep track of your energies and what works for balancing them. You can also keep track of what imbalances you have had in the past, which ensures you can navigate those imbalances more effectively if they surface again in the future.

Meditate Regularly

Meditation is an extremely useful tool when it comes to balancing your energy centers, including your third eye. Through meditation, you unify your body and your life force energy through stillness and breath, which allows you to manage your energy in a more meaningful way. Through the power of stillness and your breath, you can set any number of intentions and breathe them directly into your third eye, creating a pristine opportunity to protect yourself, cleanse yourself, or balance yourself as needed.

Aside from observational, awakening, and experiencing meditations, you can do a protection meditation as well. Protection meditations can be done by using your breath to breathe energy into a shield that you form around your third eye. This shield should be designed to protect your third eye from unwanted energy penetrating your field or being absorbed by you in any way whatsoever.

If you know you will be going into a particularly draining place, such as a place with an energy vampire or a person who tends to drain your energy, you can create a shield using your mind's eye. This shield can be built through your breath, but it should be designed to look like a mirror with the reflective portion of the mirror facing outward. This way, you experience a sort of protection that enables others' draining energy to be reflected back onto them, rather than being absorbed by yourself.

Practice Grounding Breaths

Grounding breaths are similar to meditation, except they can be done without having to meditate actively. Grounding breaths can be used when you are standing in line, driving your car, or doing other activities where actual meditation may not be possible or acceptable. There are many different grounding breath rituals you can do that allow you to fully release your unwanted energy and create a sense of calm within yourself once more.

There are three main grounding breaths you can use, depending on where you are and what you are doing. If you need to keep your wits about you but need to calm your energy field, a square breath is the best option. A square breath can be done by breathing into your diaphragm for four seconds, holding it for four seconds, breathing out for four seconds, and then holding it for four seconds. Repeat this a few times over before allowing your breath to resume a natural rhythm.

If you are able to sit down, a deeply grounding breath can be used. This deeply grounding breath allows you to create a sense of relief from your energy, but it may make you feel light-headed if you are standing or trying to focus on something. This breath is done by breathing in for a count of four, holding it for a count of seven, and breathing out for a count of eight. You should only do 5-10 of these breaths at a time, before allowing your breath to resume to its natural rhythm for a few minutes.

The third breathing rhythm you can do is a more consistent breathing routine that can help calm you without the need for holding your breath. If you have breathing issues or are pregnant, this can help stimulate calm without creating overwhelm or lightheadedness. To do this breathing rhythm, you will breathe in for a count of five and out for a count of five, deepening your breath more with each inhalation. This breathing pattern will help ground you while keeping you comfortable and focused on the present task at hand.

Take Advantage of Kundalini Yoga

Kundalini yoga is a form of yoga that was intentionally developed for working with your chakras. Other forms of yoga, such as

Hatha yoga, are excellent for balancing your energy and allowing you to feel a deep sense of peace and calm within yourself. But when it comes to specifically working with your chakras, kundalini yoga is the best.

If you choose to use kundalini yoga to balance and protect your energy, it is recommended that you do so with a kundalini yoga instructor, and not just on your own. While there are many routines you can follow on YouTube, doing so can lead to you activating and working with energy that you are not yet ready to work with. Working with a specific kundalini yoga instructor ensures that you receive access to personal guidance and spiritual support that helps you navigate those stronger energies.

If you want to do a kundalini yoga practice at home on your own, have your teacher show you a practice you can do at home. This way, the routine is designed for you specifically and will work directly on your energy field as desired. They can also discuss what to do if you end up experiencing overactive energy as a result, or if you experience something unusual with your energy. Having this information in advance, and having it tailored to your needs, ensures that you are getting everything you need from your kundalini yoga without having an unwanted experience.

Use the Emotional Freedom Technique (EFT)

Emotional freedom technique, or EFT, is a method of energy work that works similarly to acupuncture or acupressure. The idea of EFT is that you physically tap specific meridian points on your body, which are said to hold a significant amount of energy within them. You can use EFT for everything from releasing excess energy from your aura to creating protection and freedom within your third eye.

To use EFT, you need to follow five specific steps. They are as follows:

Step 1: Identifying the Issue

The issue reflects the need. If you are trying to protect your third eye, then the issue is either overactive energy or a fear of not having a well enough protected third eye chakra.

Step 2: Testing the Initial Intensity

You should always test the intensity of an issue by first rating it on a scale of 0-10, with 10 meaning the issue is extremely overwhelming or pressing. This will be your benchmark to determine how well you have tapped away your troubles.

Step 3: Setting Up Your Session

Setting up your session requires you to identify a phrase you can use to address your issue. It helps you acknowledge your issue and accept yourself in spite of the issues you are experiencing. The phrase should be something like this: "Even though I have this [fear or problem], I deeply and completely accept myself." For example, "Even though I have a fear of an overactive third eye chakra, I deeply and completely accept myself."

Step 4: The EFT Tapping Sequence

The tapping sequences require you to use your index and middle finger from your dominant hand to tap specific meridians across your body. You will tap these areas:

- The side of your non-dominant hand (small intestine meridian)
- The top of your head (governing vessel)
- Above your eyebrow (bladder meridian)
- The temple next to your eye (gallbladder meridian)
- Under your eye, on your upper cheekbone (stomach meridian)
- Under your nose, over your cupids bow (governing vessel)
- On your chin, directly under your mouth (central vessel)
- Beginning of the collarbone (kidney meridian)
- Under the arm, lower than your armpit (spleen meridian)

Repeat the tapping sequence 3-5 times, depending on how intense your problem is. Then, finish your final sequence by tapping the top of your head once again. As you tap each area, repeat your setup phrase to yourself, as this helps release the energy from those meridians and sets you up for closure from your troubles.

Step 5: Testing the Final Intensity

After you finish your tapping sequence, you need to take a few deep breaths and test yourself for intensity once more. To do this, rate the intensity of your problem from 0-10, with 10 meaning it is maximum intensity. Ideally, you should experience a less intense variety of your pain, or it should be completely eliminated. You can always repeat the sequence in a few hours or after a couple of days, until you experience full relief from your issue.

Take Advantage of Sound Healing

Sound healing is an excellent tool for healing your energy. Using the binaural beat frequency of 432Hz is excellent when it comes to healing your energy field or protecting yourself, as it is specifically designed for balance and protection. You can use a recorded frequency, but it is better if you use sound forks, crystal bowls, or other sound healing tools to help you facilitate a sound healing session. If you are not sure of how to do this, you can book a session with a practitioner and have them create a sound session specifically for protecting your third eye.

Conclusion

Congratulations on finishing this book in its entirety! While you may be done reading this book, you are likely still far from achieving the process of awakening. I can tell because a true awakening takes a significant amount of time to be fully facilitated and balanced.

I hope that reading this book has helped you to open your eyes to the reality of awakening your third eye while showing you how to do so safely and with intention. My desire is for you to be able to activate this magnificent energy center of yours in a way that feels empowering, fulfilling, and deeply comfortable. While this process may push you out of your comfort zone, it is a truly worthwhile endeavor.

After reading this book, it is important that you continue to facilitate your awakening process. Continue to ground and balance yourself as you expand your abilities. The process of awakening and working with your third eye is a never-ending journey, as there will always be more for you to learn, experience, and integrate.

It may be helpful to find a friend or a group of individuals who are also working with their third eyes. Having friends who you can share your experiences with, and who can support you along the way is a wonderful thing. While the third eye awakening is a highly personal experience, there is no reason why it has to be done entirely alone.

Remember always to trust your instinct, and to be patient in your awakening. Do what feels right and take as much time as you need. Always err on the side of caution whenever possible. You want to avoid being overwhelmed by the extensive energy that can be drawn in through your third eye. When it comes to your third eye, your intuition should always have the final say.

Thank you again for taking the time to read this book. I hope you have enjoyed it, and I wish you the best of luck on your spiritual journey!

www.ingramcontent.com/pod-product-compliance
Lightning Source LLC
LaVergne TN
LVHW011740060526
838200LV00051B/3274